Dogs

Emma Helbrough
Designed by Josephine Thompson

Illustrated by Patrizia Donaera and Uwe Mayer
Dog consultant: Emma Milne
Reading consultant: Alison Kelly, Roehampton University

Contents

Different dogs

There are lots of different kinds of dogs. Some are very big, but others are tiny. They can have long fur or short fur.

This spotted dog is called a Dalmatian.

Puppies

Mother dogs usually give birth to between six and ten puppies. They sleep close together to keep warm.

A group of puppies is called a litter.

Puppies begin to walk at two weeks old.
They like to explore as they get older.

Puppies grow their first teeth at three
weeks old and begin to eat solid food.

They start to grow their adult teeth at four
months old and like to chew things.

5

Playtime

Puppies start to play together when they are about three weeks old.

Puppies like to play-fight. They jump on top of each other to show who is strongest.

Dogs often chase each other around parks. They take turns being chased.

Some dogs live in the wild. Wolves are wild dogs. Their pups play like pet puppies.

Pet puppies chase after things for fun.

Wild pups chase too but they are learning to hunt.

In the pack

Dogs like to be with people or other dogs.

Wolves live in groups called packs.

There can be up to fifteen wolves in a pack. One of the wolves is the pack leader. The other wolves follow their leader's orders.

Pet dogs think their owner is their pack leader.

A dog greets its pack leader by licking its face.

Then it lies on its back to show it knows who is boss.

Puppies often play as if they are in a pack.

One of the puppies is always more bossy than the rest. It acts as the pack leader.

On guard

A dog's home and the area around it is called its territory.

Dogs think they own their territory, so they guard it.

They bark
when strangers
come near.

Basenjis are the
only kind of
dog that
can't bark.

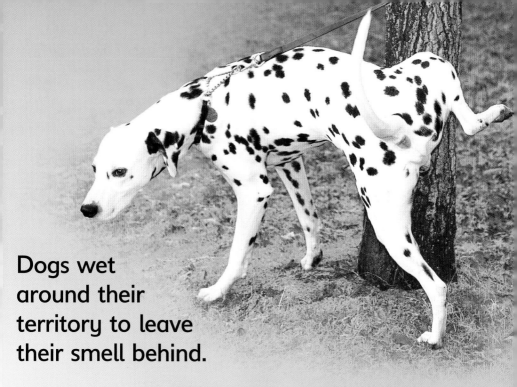

Dogs wet
around their
territory to leave
their smell behind.

When a dog sniffs an area it can tell if it
belongs to another dog.

Dogs try to take over each other's territory.

A dog sniffs a post
where another dog
has already been.

Then it wets the
post to cover up the
other dog's smell.

11

Dog talk

Dogs make lots of noises but they use their face and body to show how they feel too.

A dog wags its tail quickly when it is happy or excited.

It growls and shows its teeth when it is very angry.

It pricks its ears up when it is interested in something.

It puts its tail between its legs if it thinks it is in trouble.

WOOO 〇 〇 〇 〇

Some dogs howl if they are left alone. They are calling to their owner.

This dog wants to play. It has put its front legs down and its bottom in the air.

This is called a play-bow.

Digging

Dogs like to dig for fun but they dig for lots of other reasons too.

A mother wild dog digs a deep hole in the ground.

The hole is called a den. She crawls inside to have her pups.

The pups live inside the den while they are very young.

On a hot day, some dogs dig a hole in the ground.

Then they lie in the hole because it's cooler there.

Dogs often bury their toys to keep them safe. They dig them up when they want to play.

In the wild

Wild dogs hunt for food in packs. Their young pups stay behind in the den.

These African wild dog pups are waiting for their pack to return from hunting.

African wild dogs live in hot places, so they spend most of the day resting in the shade.

On a hunt, a pack of African wild dogs creeps up on a group of zebras.

The zebras scatter when they see the dogs. The dogs begin to chase one of the zebras.

When the zebra gets tired, the dogs catch it and gather around to eat it.

Sniffing around

Dogs have an amazing sense of smell. They can tell more about something by smelling it than by looking at it.

Dogs sniff each other when they meet.

They can tell how old another dog is and if it's a male or a female just by sniffing it.

After a dog has been given a bath, its fur smells different.

So it rolls in smelly things to cover up the new smell.

Dogs wiggle their noses when they sniff to get a better smell.

Bloodhounds have the best sense of smell. It is thousands of times better than yours.

Search and rescue

Dogs use their good sense of smell to help people find things and find other people.

At airports trained dogs sniff people's bags.

They find things that people are not allowed to take on planes, such as animals and weapons.

After an earthquake dogs help rescue teams search through the rubble.

Rescue teams use dogs to find people who are lost on mountains.

A dog can smell if someone is trapped under the snow.

The dog barks when it finds someone and the team digs them out.

21

Clever helpers

Some dogs are trained to help people who can't hear or see very well.

Hearing dogs tell their owner if they hear a sound, such as an alarm clock.

The dog touches its owner with a paw when it hears a sound.

If it hears a smoke alarm, the dog lies down to show danger.

If it hears a doorbell, the dog then leads its owner to the door.

Guide dogs help people who can't see well to travel safely.

The dogs are trained to lead their owner around things.

They learn to wait at the edge of a road until it is safe to cross.

Sheepdogs

Farmers use dogs to round up sheep in fields.

A kind of dog called a border collie is often used as a sheepdog.

This puppy will start training to be a sheepdog when it is six months old.

Sheepdogs can also be trained to round up cows, goats and even ducks!

The farmer uses a whistle and shouts to the sheepdog.

The sheepdog creeps behind the sheep and guides them to a sheep pen.

If a sheep strays from the group, the sheepdog runs over to guide it back again.

Sled dogs

Teams of dogs pull sleds across the snow. Some people use them to travel around. Other people race them for fun.

Each dog wears a harness which clips onto a long line.

Then the line is joined to the front of the sled.

The person who drives the sled is called a musher.

Sled dogs get hungry after running a race.
They eat six times as much food as pet dogs.

The dogs often wear
socks to protect their
paws from the snow.

The musher shouts
"hike" or "let's go"
to start the dogs.

Dog families

If a mother and a father dog look exactly the same, their puppies look the same too. They are called purebreds.

These old English sheepdog puppies will grow up to look like their parents.

If a mother and a father dog don't look the same...

...their puppies look like a mixture of both of them.

Dogs that are a mixture of different kinds are called mixed breeds.

Mixed breed dogs are often more healthy and live longer than purebred dogs.

Glossary of dog words

Here are some of the words in this book you might not know. This page tells you what they mean.

 pups - another word for puppies. Wild dog puppies are often called pups.

 pack - a group of dogs. Wild dogs live in packs.

 pack leader - the dog that is in charge of all the other dogs in a pack.

 territory - the place where a dog lives. Dogs guard their territory.

 den - the place where wild pups are born and live when they are very small.

 harness - a special strap that a dog sometimes wears.

 sheepdog - a dog that is trained to round up sheep.

Websites to visit

You can visit exciting websites to find out more about dogs.

To visit these websites, go to the Usborne Quicklinks Website at **www.usborne-quicklinks.com** Read the internet safety guidelines, and then type the keywords "**beginners dogs**".

The websites are regularly reviewed and the links in Usborne Quicklinks are updated. However, Usborne Publishing is not responsible, and does not accept liability, for the content or availability of any website other than its own. We recommend that children are supervised while on the internet.

This pet dog has been rubbed dry after a bath.

Index

Acknowledgements

Photographic manipulation: John Russell

Photo credits
The publishers are grateful to the following for permission to reproduce material:
© **Africa Imagery:** 16 (Roger de la Harpe); © **Ardea:** 11, 24 (John Daniels); © **Frank Lane Picture Agency:** 8 (Tim Fitzharris/Minden Pictures), 23 (Klein/Hubert/FotoNatura); © **Getty Images:** cover (Martin Harvey), 29 (Patricia Doyle), 1 (Gary Randall), 2-3 (Geoff du Feu), 19 (Dag Sundberg); © **ImageState:** 28; © **Leeson Photos:** 7 (Tom & Pat Leeson); © **NHPA:** 4 (E.A.Janes), 9 (Henry Ausloos); © **Powerstock:** 21 (Bob Winsett/Index Stock Imagery); © **Richard Schiller:** 26-27; © **Warren Photographic:** 10, 18, 31 (Jane Burton); 13 (Kim Taylor); © **Workbookstock:** 15 (Lori Adamski-Peek)

Every effort has been made to trace and acknowledge ownership of copyright. If any rights have been omitted, the publishers offer to rectify this in any subsequent editions following notification.

Sun, moon and stars

Farm animals

Elizabeth I

TRASH AND RECYCLING

Dogs

Horses and ponies

Spiders

Planes

Ancient Greeks

Cats

VOLCANOES

DINOSAURS

Your Body

Armor

Sharks

Celts

Vikings

Castles

How flowers grow

Digging up History

Living in space

Caterpillars and Butterflies

Ballet

Pirates

Egyptians

Eggs and Chicks

Romans

Weather

Tadpoles and frogs

Why do we eat?

Under the sea

Bears

Aztecs

TRUCKS

Night Animals

Firefighters

Antarctica

Bugs

COWBOYS

Planet Earth